ESCAPING MEDIOCRITY

WITH THE

FOUR WEEK QTR

NICK WEBB SR.

Forward:

From Enthusiasm to Achievement: Learning from My Past

I used to experience a curious phenomenon each September: a surge of energy and enthusiasm for tackling grand goals. Yet, by November, I'd often forget what those goals were or why they mattered. This cycle repeated year after year, driven by a burst of ambition that fizzled out as quickly as it had arrived.

September seemed to bring out the dreamer in me, with big ideas—some brilliant, others less so. But as I dug into how to turn these dreams into reality, I'd frequently encounter obstacles that dampened my enthusiasm and left me questioning my ability to succeed.

It wasn't until I read "Think and Grow Rich" by Napoleon Hill that I began to understand why my goals often went unfulfilled. More importantly, I discovered insights into how I had achieved success in other areas of my life, particularly in sports like football and basketball.

Growing up as one of seven children, and second to the youngest, I was primarily raised by my mother while my father was absent. Neither of my parents had a background in sports, but I developed a passion for football at an early age. I played with the neighborhood kids every day, regardless of the weather—rain, sleet, or snow (being from Illinois mostly snow).

What set me apart was more than just enthusiasm; I noticed I was faster and more athletic compared to my peers. The same held true for basketball, which I started playing at the age of 13. Despite being self-taught, I quickly excelled, earning accolades, invitations, and scholarship offers.

The secret to my success in sports wasn't merely passion; it was my relentless dedication to practice. I committed to playing every day, without exception. My routine involved going to the court with my little brother each morning, focusing on ball-handling and cardio. After a few runs with the neighborhood kids, we'd head home for lunch, only to return to the court for hours of shooting practice. I set a personal benchmark of hitting 300 shots before calling it a day, often playing games with older kids and adults to further sharpen my skills.

This daily grind taught me the fundamentals of time management, performance standards, and consistent measurement. It was my introduction to time blocking, staying focused on the task at hand, and the relentless pursuit of attainable goals.

These experiences laid the groundwork for understanding how to turn enthusiasm into tangible results. They showed me the importance of daily effort, consistent practice, and setting clear performance standards. By applying these lessons to other areas of life, I learned that achieving goals is not just about having a grand vision but also about the disciplined, daily actions that drive success.

If you're someone who's driven to boost your productivity and efficiency, looking to balance family responsibilities with your personal ambitions, or ready to finally build that successful business and achieve financial independence, then the Four Week Quarter program is made for you. This program is your blueprint for turning motivation into real, lasting success.

Contents

Chapter 1:

What is the Four Week Quarter?

The 4 WEEK Quarter is a program that seeks to challenge the way we traditionally look at goal achievement by introducing, incremental actions, time management, milestones, and measurement.

This program is specifically designed for those of us who:

- Find it challenging to manage time effectively and often feel overwhelmed by the competing demands of work and personal life.

- Lack a clear and structured approach to setting and achieving meaningful goals.

- Frequently juggle multiple tasks, leaving you feeling like there just isn't enough time in the day.

- Struggle with balancing personal goals alongside family responsibilities and obligations.

- Have difficulty prioritizing tasks or managing time effectively between your primary job and your side hustle.

- Have trouble maintaining momentum and focus on long-term goals.

This program is here to help you reclaim control, find balance, and make lasting progress in every area of your life.

This program illustrates how you can accomplish in 4 weeks what most people can't accomplish in 1 year in respect to our goals by focusing on:

- Your most impactful goals

- The milestones and action items that make up that goal

- Time management by way of time blocking

- Active evaluation and measurement of weekly performance

In the 4 Week Quarter, every week is a month, every day is broken down into 3 separate days. The chart below shows how the 4 Week Quarter differs from our standard structure of living.

Time Period	Traditional View	4 Week Quarter View	Description
1 Day	One 24-hour Period (12 AM - 11:59 PM)	Three Q-Days: Q-Day 1: 6AM - 12PM Q-Day 2: 12PM - 6PM Q-Day 3: 6PM - Midnight	By time blocking and creating 3 separate days within one day, this allows us to force our action items into certain periods of our days. This creates abstract deadlines that push our urgency. By dedicating specific time blocks to individual tasks, you minimize distractions and increase concentration on the task at hand and reduces the likelihood of multitasking.

As mentioned above, the Four Week Quarter program is comprised of 4 critical processes.

The Four Week Quarter program and all of its processes, tools, and templates are available in a simple easy to use application in your app store; we suggest that you download the application as you go through your first Four Week Quarter program. The app is a step-by-step repeatable process that walks you through the build of your Four Week Quarter, your goals, your daily actions, and your weekly review scores.

Crafting your most impactful goal:

Characteristics of a goal is that it's "specific", "measurable", "achievable", "relevant", and it's "time-bound".

- Being specific about your goal means to clearly define what you want to achieve. For example, instead of saying "I want to be healthier," a specific goal would be "I want to exercise for 30 minutes five times a week."

- Ensuring your goal is measurable would-be providing criteria for tracking progress and determining when the goal has been achieved. This involves quantifying the outcome, such as "increase sales by 15% within six months."

- An achievable goal ensures that the goal is realistic and attainable given your current resources and constraints. It should challenge you but remain within the realm of possibility. The goal that you choose for the next 4 weeks should be relevant, it should align with your broader objectives, values, and long-term aspirations.

- A relevant goal is one that fits with your overall vision and has significance to you.

- At lastly, your goal should be time-bound; we take care of this given the nature of the Four Week Quarter program, but in thinking of your goal it should be something that's attainable now.

With those things in mind, think of the milestone or goal that if achieved now would have the most critical impact in your life; either that goal or a modified version of that goal is what you'll focus on for the next four weeks.

The breakdown of your goal to high level milestones & small bite-sized action items:

Now that you have your goal crafted, how close are you to achieving that goal? Whether you're close to fulfilling this goal or miles away, you'll likely cross many milestones that get you closer to fulfilling it. In order to quantify if you're getting close to your goal or going in the right direction, we must document these milestones.

The process of breaking down your goal into high level milestones and in-turn breaking down those milestones into to small bite-sized action it items is the most pivotal process in the 4 Week quarter as it sets the stage for the work and hedges against burn out and feeling overwhelmed.

Time-Blocking (3 Q-Days in 1 Day):

The Four Week Quarter uses a process that allows its users to time-block or compartmentalize the day into 3 specific blocks of times in which we use to schedule the actions - we call these Q-Days. Each 24 hours consists of 3 blocks of time (3 Q-Days):

Q-Day 1: 6AM - 12PM

Yes, its true - the early bird does get the worm. Here is one tiny seemingly insignificant thing but actually huge nugget I've learned in life - we all know at this point about the rat race, but what we don't realize is the key to getting settled into and stuck in the rat race is that the time and energy maintaining the race expends on our mental, physical, and emotional state is a direct correlation to not putting in time and effort into the places that would allow us to escape the rate race. Hence the 4 Week Quarter - a strategic process of incrementally stealing back your time to then use it for the escape. We must do life and on top of that, work on our goals.

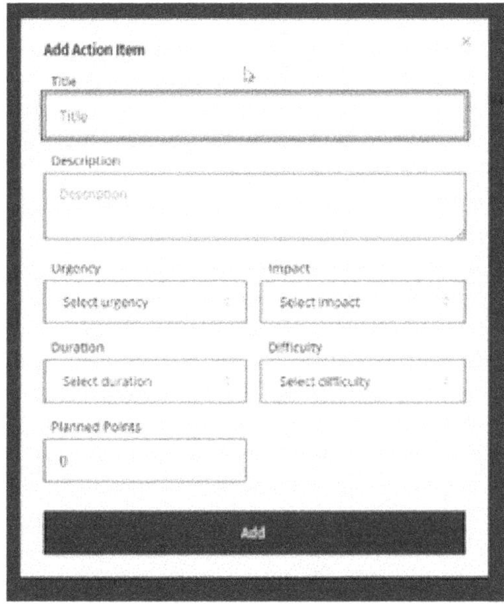

I'm a father of two amazing son's Nick Jr (8), and Langston (7) and have them 50% as well as a budding business I'm building. Waking up early is key to having some quiet time to myself to focus on getting milestones completed before I need to get the boys up, cook breakfast, and get them ready for school, camp, or whatever they have going on that day.

This early rising is much more than quiet time; it sets the stage for a focused day. During this time block (Q-Day 1), I set my schedule for my 4-week quarter daily action items during the 6AM - 7:30AM, and depending on my work schedule I may be able to complete tasks between 10:30 - 12PM. Your Q-Day 1 being efficient also calls for a decent bed time the night before - which could mean a lifestyle change for some of us.

You will need to take this same approach when scheduling out your week in advance; be realistic about what you can get done.

Q-Day 2: 12PM - 6PM

This time-block is a challenging one if you have other priorities in your life as this is the middle of a workday for most of us. During this time, it's important not to schedule large action items; if scheduling things during this time they should be limited to small actions e.g. make 5 calls to clients or complete and send over NDA. The actions scheduled during Q-Day 2 should be very specific tasks that have a beginning and end with an expected output.

Q-Day 3: 6PM – 12AM

6PM - 12AM is a busy part of the day for me and my family on the days that I have my sons; the work day is basically over but the boys are out of school/ camp, they have homework, Kumon, baseball, basketball, school projects, we have to eat, and not to mention just spending quality time with them.

Understanding your schedule, knowing your priorities, and building your weekly plan off of true capacity is another critical aspect of succeeding in your Four Week Quarter program. On Tuesdays and Thursdays, I don't have my sons; with that said I make sure to ensure my workday is light and client meetings are early so I can overload those days with 4-week quarter actions; these along with weekends where I don't have my sons will be my most productive days.

Active measurement and performance evaluation:

"That which is measured is improved". At the end of your week (Saturday evening) is when you should review your week; it's important to take a moment to score each Q-Day at the end of each time-block throughout the week. For example, on Monday around

11:45 AM, I would suggest you take a moment and ask yourself the measurement question -"Did I complete this Q-Days tasks as planned".

You'll be ranking yourself on a scale of (0% to 100% with '0%' being "not at all", and '100%' being "you killed it and have the exact output you planned on"). You'll do the same measurement at the end of each Q-day of each week.

By the end of the week, you'll review your week's performance which will be presented as % complete. Any % complete over 70% means you're on the path to completing your goals.

(The breakdown in Q-Days, active measurement, weighted scoring, and algorithm's will all be available in the Four Week Quarter application.)

Rules to measurement:

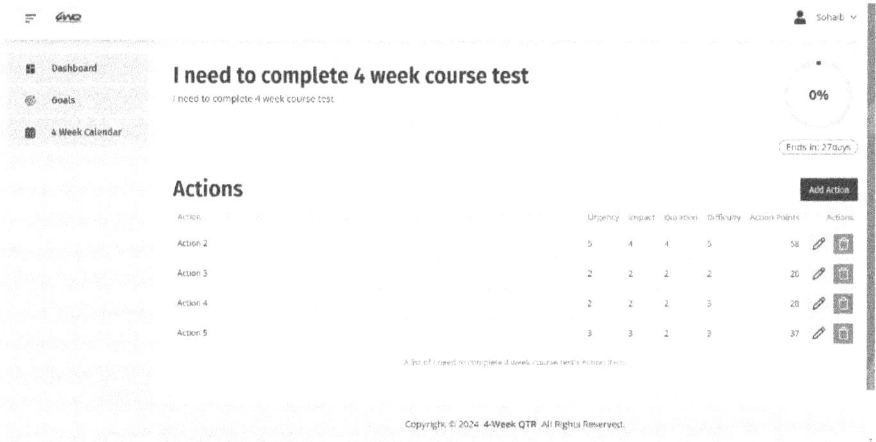

- o Each 1 Day is split into 3 Q-Days

- o Each Q-Day will need at least 1 "Action Item" planned.

- o Each Action Item will have an overall ranking (0% - 100%) for users to measure their performance for that Action.

    - Each Q-Day will show 3 numbers after you've ranked the day

1. The % that you've ranked that day (0% - 100%)

2. Total Points Possible (in Green)

3. Calculated Points earned (in Yellow)

o Users should take time to measure each action at the end of that specified Q-Day (e.g., 11:45AM for Q-Day 1, 5:45 PM for Q-Day 2, right before bedtime for Q-Day 3).

o At the end of each week, you'll review each Q-Days total points earned and % complete.

Every week completed gives opportunity to score 21 Q-Days of work effort targeted on your goal. We're suggesting that if you can complete at least 70% of your planned actions over a 4-week span, you'll accomplish more in that four weeks than others will in a given year when it comes to goal achievement.

Chapter 2

Overcoming Common Pitfalls

"Success is often just on the other side of our most common mistakes—so treat each pitfall as a plot twist, not the final scene." Starting strong on your Four-Week Quarter journey feels empowering, doesn't it? That sense of purpose and direction, knowing you're setting yourself up for success—there's nothing like it.

But let's be real for a minute: no matter how committed you are, life has a way of testing your resolve. You'll hit bumps in the road, and even the most focused individuals face challenges that threaten to throw them off course. The secret to staying on track isn't just about sticking to the plan—it's about anticipating common setbacks and having solid strategies to bounce back when they happen.

The Burnout Trap

Pitfall: Burnout is sneaky. You push yourself hard, aiming to get the most out of every minute, but before you know it, you're mentally and physically exhausted. Even with the best time management in place, trying to do too much, too fast will catch up with you.

Solution:

- Pace Yourself: Don't try to sprint through your goals. This is a marathon, not a race. Consistency will get you much further than burning yourself out. Stick to your action plan and avoid overcommitting.

- Schedule Breaks: Listen, breaks aren't a luxury—they're a necessity. Building in time to pause and recharge is key to sustaining productivity and creativity. A five-minute breather between your Q-Days can make all the difference.

- Monitor Your Energy: Pay attention to how you're feeling throughout the day. If you notice your productivity slipping, switch to a lighter task or take a quick power nap. Those small adjustments can keep burnout from creeping up on you.

- Celebrate Small Wins: Recognizing progress—no matter how small—keeps your motivation alive. It's easy to focus on what's left to do, but give yourself credit for what you've already achieved.

Procrastination and Lack of Focus

Pitfall: It's easy to procrastinate when a task feels overwhelming. And let's not even get started on distractions—whether it's your phone blowing up with notifications or emails pulling your attention away from what really matters.

Solution:

- Break It Down: The Four-Week Quarter is built on breaking your goals into manageable chunks for a reason. If something feels too big, break it down even further. Keep it simple.

- Use the "2-Minute Rule": If it takes two minutes or less to complete, just knock it out. This keeps little tasks from piling up and frees up mental space.

- Limit Distractions: When you need to focus, cut the noise. Turn on "Do Not Disturb" or use apps that block distracting websites.

- Stick to Time Blocking: Your Q-Day structure is there to keep you focused. When each block is dedicated to a specific task, it makes it easier to avoid procrastinating and stay productive.

The Perfectionism Trap

Pitfall: Perfectionism can be paralyzing. You get caught up in trying to make everything flawless, and before you know it, progress has slowed to a crawl.

Solution:

- Set Time Limits for Tasks: Give yourself a set amount of time for each task, and once it's up, move on. Done is always better than perfect.

- Embrace Imperfection: You don't need to get everything 100% right—just moving forward is what matters. Progress over perfection, every time.

- Use Feedback Loops: Build small check-ins or feedback sessions into your process. This lets you refine your work as you go, rather than waiting until you think it's perfect to move forward.

Losing Motivation Midway

Pitfall: You start out strong, but somewhere in the middle, life happens, and you lose that initial fire. It's normal, but it can be hard to stay on track when you're juggling everything else.

Solution:

- Revisit Your 'Why': Remind yourself why you set these goals in the first place. What's the bigger picture? How will achieving this change your life for the better?

- Use Visual Reminders: Keep your goals visible—whether it's a sticky note on your mirror or a vision board. Visual cues can be powerful motivators.

- Track Your Progress: There's nothing more motivating than seeing how far you've come. Regularly review your weekly scores to stay grounded in your progress.

- Reward Yourself: Don't underestimate the power of a good reward. Knowing there's something waiting for you at the end of a milestone can keep you going.

Balancing Competing Priorities

Pitfall: Life doesn't hit pause just because you're working toward a goal. You still have to juggle work, family, and personal responsibilities.

Solution:

- Set Boundaries: Be upfront with those around you about the time you've carved out for your goals. This sets expectations and minimizes interruptions.

- Use "Theme Days": Assign specific days to certain areas of focus. Maybe weekends are for personal goals, and weekdays are for professional ones.

- Batch Similar Tasks: Grouping similar activities can boost efficiency. If you've got calls to make, schedule them all-in one-time block instead of spreading them out.

- Be Realistic: Some weeks will be busier than others. It's okay to adjust your workload when life gets hectic—just get back on track as soon as you can.

Fear of Failure

Pitfall: Fear of failure can stop you in your tracks. The thought of not hitting your goal can make you hesitate or avoid tasks altogether. But I say, the thought of not going after the life you want is much more scare of failure.

Solution:

- Reframe Failure: Failure is part of the process. Each setback teaches you something valuable that brings you closer to success.

- Set 'Failure Goals': Instead of avoiding mistakes, aim to learn from them. Each misstep offers insights that'll help you in the future.

- Track Progress, Not Perfection: It's okay if not every day is perfect. What matters is that you're making progress, even if it's not always smooth.

Inconsistent Measurement

Pitfall: If you're not consistently tracking your progress, it's easy to lose sight of where you stand. You may think you're doing better (or worse) than you actually are.

Solution:

- Make Measurement a Habit: At the end of each block, review your Q-Days. It only takes a few minutes, but it'll keep you accountable.

- Use the Four-Week Quarter App: The app makes it easy to log scores and track your progress, helping you stay on top of things.

- Focus on Patterns: Some days will be tougher than others. What matters is the overall trend. Look for patterns to gauge your long-term trajectory.

- Adjust as Needed: Weekly reviews give you the chance to tweak your approach. Flexibility is key to success.

Lack of Accountability

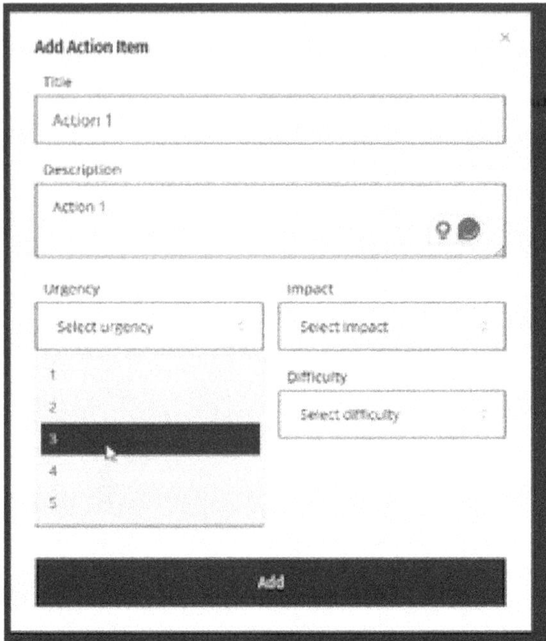

Pitfall: Without someone to hold you accountable, it's easy to push deadlines or let tasks slip.

Solution:

- Create an Accountability Partner: Find someone who can check in on your progress regularly—a friend, colleague, or mentor.

- Join a community: Connect with others working through the Four-Week Quarter. Sharing both wins and setbacks helps build motivation.

- Use Self-Accountability Tools: The Four-Week Quarter app offers built-in accountability with scoring and reviews to keep you on track.

- Reward and Reflect: Set small rewards for hitting milestones, and take time to reflect on what's working. This keeps you motivated and learning as you go.

Overcoming these common pitfalls isn't about perfection—it's about being prepared, adaptable, and consistent. There will be tough days, but success is about staying committed to the process. Keep moving forward, even when it feels challenging. By the end of your Four-Week Quarter, you'll have achieved more than you thought possible and built the habits that set you up for lasting success.

Chapter 3

Defining Your Most Impactful Goal

If you're diving into this book, it's likely because you're driven by the desire to stand out at work, secure that promotion, achieve financial stability, or make the most of your time and performance. The Four Week Quarter attracts a community of go-getters—people who are eager to create something of their own, seek financial freedom, and want the flexibility to work on their own terms. We have that inner fire to turn our passions into profit.

The Four Week Quarter is all about using proven strategies to bring more structure to our daily routines, making room for self-improvement and personal goals.

Have you ever found yourself thinking, "If I had (fill in the blank), I could be exactly where I need to be"? This question is more than a moment of wishful thinking—it's a crucial step in understanding your aspirations, needs, and current capabilities. By carefully examining these elements, you can select a goal that will have the greatest impact on both your personal and professional life.

By developing a comprehensive action plan, you can effectively focus on achieving a goal that will bring the greatest personal and professional fulfillment within the next 4 weeks.

To set yourself up for success in your next Four Week Quarter, it's vital to start with a thoughtful, structured approach to goal setting. This means aligning your goal with your broader vision and ensuring it is specific, measurable, achievable, relevant, and time-bound (SMART). Here's how to tackle this crucial task:

Step 1. Create a vision statement; a vision statement is a forward-looking declaration of your organization's or your personal long-term aspirations. It serves as a guiding star, providing direction and inspiration as well as helps align efforts and communicates the overarching purpose and direction.

In creating a vision statement, you'll want to envision the future; imagine where you see yourself in the next year - what is the ultimate impact or legacy you want to create? This is a time of immense reflection where you'll need to find a quiet space and really reflect on what you want within the next year. This is the time to set ambitious goals - think about the highest level of achievement you aspire to; what does success look like in the long run?

When I started my first Four Week Quarter program, my vision statement read as follows, "In the next 10 years my consulting firm will be an active government prime contractor". My vision statement is:

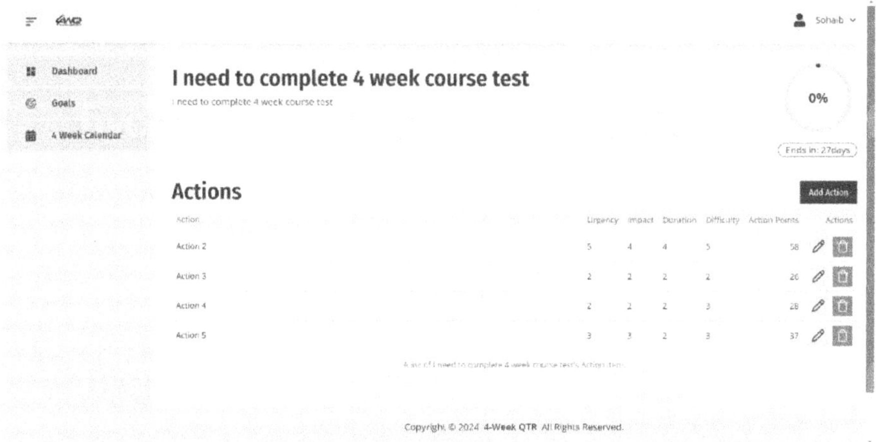

- o   Specific in that it mentioned a partnership with a specific customer base.

- o   Measurable as there are specific steps to become a prime government contractor.

- o   Achievable based on the time I allotted myself and proven processes to become a prime contractor.

- o   Relevant as it builds onto my current business.

o   Time-bound as it mentions 10 years giving myself a realistic time frame.

One of the first major goals that I aligned with my visions statement that I set was "Over the next 4 weeks I will take the necessary steps to effectively and successfully partner with a prime contractor and sell services to the government. This goal takes into account that there will be steps to partner with a prime as well as knowledge I'll need to acquire and skills I'll need to pick up along the way; these steps, knowledge, and skills will be detailed in my action items that fill my daily schedule.

Be extremely truthful with yourself during this session of analysis. Assess your current situation or the current state of your organization.

o   What are your strengths, what unique capabilities do you possess that could help you achieve a significant goal?

o   What are your weaknesses, recognize any limitations or areas for improvement. Being aware of these can help in selecting a goal that is realistic and achievable. Don't underestimate how powerful this awareness is; this honest evaluation will put you in a place to know the exact types of partnerships or employees that you'll need to eventually bring into your organization.

o   What are your opportunities, look for opportunities within your industry, community, or personal life that align with your strengths and mission. What knowledge, relationships, or opportunities can you capitalize on right now?

o   What are your threats, assess potential challenges that could hinder your progress. This helps in choosing a goal that you can realistically pursue given the potential obstacles.

Use your honest assessment of your strengths, weaknesses, opportunities, and threats to break down and state potential milestone and goal statements. What information specifically came out of your analysis of weaknesses, threats, and opportunities?

Identify and determine the gaps between your current state and your envisioned future. What needs to change to achieve your vision? These gaps will give you the exact goals that you'll need to focus on over the next 4 weeks.

With the work you've just done, you're now ready to craft your vision statement, you'll want to

1. Ensure that the statement is inspiring, motivating, and evoke your passion and commitment.

2. Keep the statement concise and straightforward - it should be easy to remember.

3. Reflect on your unique identity - incorporate elements that reflect your unique identity and show what makes you or your organization distinct.

Now that you have a clear and concise vision statement, you can craft the one goal that you'll focus on over the next 4 weeks. Where will this one (at the most 2 goals) come from? They'll stem from the information and analysis that you've gained from the exercises to get to your vision statement.

For example, if your vision statement is "I want to gain back the confidence I had when I was younger by ensuring I'm at on the correct path in all aspects of life, physical fitness, financial stability, emotionally, and spiritually". One of your 4 Week Quarter Goals might be "Lose 8 lbs. over the next 4 weeks".

Take this time to draft your top 1 or 2 most critical goals that you'll want to achieve over the next 4 weeks - the goal must be specific, succinct, measurable, and time boxed. You can utilize the Four Week Quarter app to document this goal.

Documenting only one (at most two) goal is also very important for your ability to stay focused; we're going to break this goal down into multiple actionable daily tasks so it's important that you'll be able to keep a one-track mind.

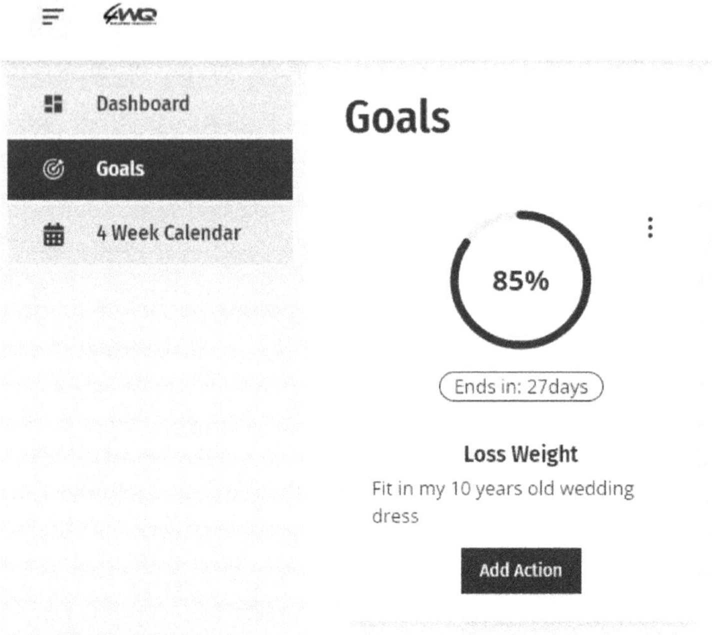

Remember, the daily tasks and action items that you'll need to complete will be in conjunction with your everyday life responsibilities - the way we'll keep you focused is to ensure we're being realistic in what and how much can be done in a 24-hour period.

Do you have your top goal documented?

Is it specific? Is it measurable?

Is it time boxed?

Great, before moving into the next chapter, take a moment to sit and visualize that this goal has been achieved. See yourself in three months; what does your day-to-day life look like if you were to achieve this goal?

Chapter 4

Knowing Your Goal Make-Up

Now that you have your 1 (at most 2) goal(s) that you're going to focus on for your first 4 Week Quarter we now have to understand and list out what actions will need to be completed to fulfill this goal. What this implies is that you understand what it takes to get to your goal or you're willing to do the research to understand how to complete your goal.

Big goals can seem daunting, but breaking them down into smaller, manageable tasks makes them more approachable and provides a clear path forward.

To keep you on track, you'll convert your overarching goal into a "Weekly Action Statement." This statement outlines what needs to be accomplished each week to hit your four-week target. Weekly Action Statements are effective because they are straightforward, focused, and ensure accountability - they keep you locked-in on the things you must complete right now.

I'll use the same example goal "Lose 4 lbs. over the next 4 weeks"; the way I would break down this goal is to understand what is needed from me to lose 8 lbs. in 4 weeks - this will take discipline diet down to measuring daily macronutrients, a constant work out plan, and ensuring I get enough sleep.

My daily "Actions" for the goal of "losing 4 lbs. in 4 weeks" are as such:

- 4 Week Goal Statement: "Lose 4 lbs. in the next 4 weeks"

- Weekly Action Statement: "Lose 1 lb. this week"

- Daily Action Items:

- o   Document weight.

- o   Complete 4 intense workouts each week (for me, these are HIT workouts)

- o   Consume 200 - 250 grams of carbohydrates from healthy sources every day (Sunday - Saturday)

- o   Consume 199 grams of proteins from healthy sources every day (Sunday - Saturday)

- o   Consume 83 grams of healthy fats every day (Sunday - Saturday)

- o   In the bed by 10 PM every day (Sunday - Saturday)

The principle here is similar to the idea that "if you focus on the pennies, the dollars will take care of themselves." By breaking your goal into manageable daily and weekly tasks and consistently executing these tasks, you'll naturally progress toward achieving your goal.

By breaking your goal down into small bite-sized chunks of impactful actions pointed at one goal, and then consistently completing these actions each and every day - the only end result is a completed goal.

In our Four Week Quarter Program, aiming to complete at least 70% of your daily actions will often result in accomplishing in four weeks what most people achieve in an entire year. This focus and consistency create momentum and drive.

Now it's time to break down your goal into small action items. This exercise can take some time as you'll need to know the detail of what it takes to achieve said goal. Below are steps you can take to complete your list of action items. (The 4 Week Quarter application allows you to document all of your goals, action items, scores, and performance measurements).

a.   Identify High-Level Milestones: Start by listing the major milestones you need to hit to achieve your goal.

b. After gathering a list of 5 - 10 high-level milestones, Decompose Milestones: For each high-level milestone, break it down into smaller, actionable tasks. The goal is to make each task as specific and manageable as possible. Then repeat this process for each high-level milestone that you've created.

  o Ask yourself, "Is this task as detailed as it can be?" If it is, you've established your initial list of action items.

  o The final list of action items that you detailed out need to be documented in the 4 Week Quarter application so they can be scored and tracked on your timeline.

Dealing with New Insights:

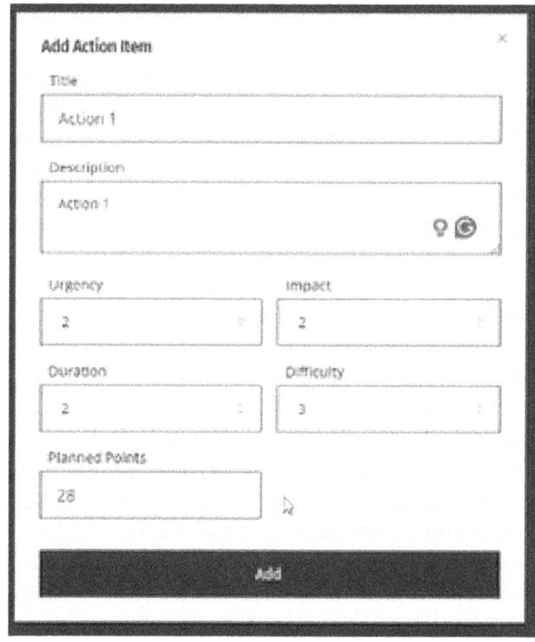

You might discover additional information or steps needed as you work towards your goal—what we call "Forced Enlightenment." This is when your pursuit of success leads you to new knowledge or perspectives that weren't initially apparent. This isn't a setback but a sign that you're progressing and learning. When encountering new knowledge, it's important not to get discouraged, this is only proof that you're doing the work that will get you to where you want to be.

Incorporate this new information into your action plan. Adjust your tasks and milestones as needed. Embrace this process, as it will enhance your focus, knowledge, and clarity.

By committing to daily action items, you'll build momentum and gain enthusiasm. Over time, you'll find yourself not only closer to your goal but also more disciplined and confident in your path forward. Self-discipline and commitment are powerful tools in achieving your objectives.

Chapter 5

Mindset and Motivation

"Motivation gets you moving, but mindset keeps you going when motivation takes a day off." When it comes to achieving your goals with the Four-Week Quarter, it's not just about the tactics, the to-do lists, or how you break down your time. It all begins up here—in your mind.

Your mindset and the fuel behind your motivation are the two factors that determine whether you keep pushing when things get hard or throw in the towel. In this chapter, we're going to dig deep into how the way you think shapes your success and how to build up the kind of motivation that keeps you going, even when the path gets rough.

The Power of Mindset: Fixed vs. Growth Thinking

How you approach challenges, setbacks, and wins is a direct reflection of your mindset. Psychologists talk about two main types:

- o Fixed Mindset: If you've got a fixed mindset, you tend to believe that your skills and intelligence are what they are, and there's not much room for growth. When failure shows up, people with this mindset often chalk it up to not having what it takes.

- o Growth Mindset: On the flip side, a growth mindset sees every challenge as an opportunity to get better. You understand that effort leads to progress, and failures are just stepping stones on the path forward.

Why It Matters

When you're working within a Four-Week Quarter, consistency and adaptability are key. A growth mindset is what helps you stay resilient when things don't go according to plan. It empowers you to face challenges, learn from mistakes, and most importantly, keep moving.

Building a Growth Mindset

Here's how to make the shift from fixed thinking to growth thinking:

- Embrace Challenges: See roadblocks as a chance to level up your skills. Instead of dodging them, face them head-on.

- Reframe Failures: Instead of saying, "I'm not good at this," switch your thinking to "I'm just not there yet." Focus on the process of learning rather than being fixated on the end result.

- Celebrate Effort, Not Just Results: Acknowledge the work you put in, even if the result isn't picture-perfect. Consistently showing up builds habits that will pay off down the line.

- Surround Yourself with Growth-Oriented People: Your circle matters. Make sure you're connected to people who challenge you to be better and who are focused on growth themselves.

Understanding Motivation: Intrinsic vs. Extrinsic Drivers

There are two main kinds of motivation that get people moving:

- Intrinsic Motivation: This comes from within. It's about personal satisfaction—like the joy of learning a new skill or the pride that comes with reaching a personal milestone.

- Extrinsic Motivation: This is driven by outside rewards—things like promotions, recognition, or financial incentives.

Why Both Matter

While intrinsic motivation tends to last longer, sometimes those external rewards are what you need to kick things into gear. The trick is to balance both. Use the external rewards to get started, but rely on your internal drive to keep going over the long haul.

Creating Meaningful Motivation: Find Your 'Why'

Understanding why you want to achieve a goal gives your effort meaning. Without a strong "why," it's easy to lose steam when things get hard.

How to Find Your 'Why':

- Reflect on Your Values: What's most important to you? When your goals align with your core values, you'll find deeper meaning in the work you're doing.

- Think Long-Term: What's the bigger picture? How will reaching this goal impact your life in the future?

- Use the 5 Whys Method: For every goal, ask yourself "Why?" five times to dig into its deeper motivation.

- Visualize Success: Imagine what your life looks like once you've achieved your goal. That mental picture becomes a motivator that keeps you focused.

Overcoming Motivation Dips

Even the most motivated people hit those moments where they just don't feel it. The key is to recognize when your motivation is dipping and have a game plan to get back on track.

Practical Tips for Regaining Motivation:

- Break It Down: When you're feeling overwhelmed, focus on the next small step rather than the entire goal.

- Revisit Your Wins: Look back on what you've already accomplished to remind yourself how far you've come.

- Switch Up Your Environment: Sometimes a change of scenery—whether it's working from a different spot or shaking up your routine—can give your energy a boost.

- Find an Accountability Partner: Having someone to check in with keeps you on your toes and ensures you stay committed.

The Role of Habits in Sustaining Motivation

Motivation might get you started, but it's habits that keep you going. Building consistent routines around your goals means you don't have to rely on willpower alone, which can wear out over time.

How to Build Productive Habits:

- Anchor New Habits to Existing Ones: Attach new behaviors to habits you already have. For example, if you start every day with a cup of coffee, use that time to review your goals.

- Start Small: Don't aim for perfection right away. Consistency is key. Working on a task for just 10 minutes a day adds up.

- Track Your Progress: Use the Four-Week Quarter app to monitor your habits. Seeing your daily wins keeps your motivation high.

- Reward Yourself: Celebrate small milestones to reinforce positive behavior.

Dealing with Negative Self-Talk and Limiting Beliefs

One of the biggest barriers to motivation is the negative chatter that goes on in your head. Recognizing and challenging these limiting beliefs is crucial if you want to keep up your momentum.

How to Manage Negative Self-Talk:

- Practice Mindfulness: Pay attention to your thoughts without getting caught up in them. When negative thoughts pop up, acknowledge them, then let them pass.

- Use Positive Affirmations: Replace that inner criticism with statements that uplift and empower you. Say things like, "I'm fully capable of achieving my goals."

- Challenge Limiting Beliefs: Ask yourself, "Is this really true?" Most of our doubts are based on assumptions, not facts.

- Focus on What You Can Control: Shift your energy toward the actions you can take, rather than stressing about things beyond your control.

Motivation Through Visualization and Affirmations

Visualization is a powerful tool. When you picture your success in detail, it builds your confidence and reduces fear, making the goal feel more achievable.

How to Use Visualization Effectively:

- Set Time Aside Daily: Spend 5–10 minutes each day visualizing yourself reaching your goals.

- Engage All Your Senses: Make the experience as vivid as possible. Imagine the sights, sounds, and emotions tied to your success.

- Combine Visualization with Affirmations: Reinforce your mental images with positive affirmations like, "I'm motivated and focused on my goals."

- Write a Letter to Your Future Self: Describe what your life looks like after achieving your goal. This solidifies your vision and strengthens your motivation.

Building a Resilient Mindset: Grit and Perseverance

Motivation is what gets you moving, but resilience—your ability to keep going when things get tough—is what ensures you reach the finish line.

How to Build Resilience:

- Adopt a Long-Term Perspective: Setbacks are part of the process. Keep your focus on the bigger picture and remember that challenges are temporary.

- Practice Self-Compassion: Don't be too hard on yourself when things don't go as planned. Self-compassion fuels resilience; self-criticism drains it.

- Develop Mental Toughness: Push yourself slightly beyond your comfort zone each day. Over time, these small challenges will build your grit and confidence.

- Celebrate Progress, Not Perfection: Focus on how far you've come rather than how far you still need to go. Progress is the real measure of success.

Using Accountability as a Motivator

Accountability is one of the strongest motivators. When someone else is expecting an update from you, you're far more likely to stay on track.

How to Build Accountability:

- Partner Up: Share your goals with a friend, mentor, or coach, and schedule regular check-ins.

- Join a Group: Being part of a community with similar goals can help you stay focused and supported.

- Use Technology: Utilize the Four-Week Quarter app to set reminders, track progress, and review your performance.

- Set Public Goals: Share your goals with others on social media or in your inner circle. Public accountability is powerful.

Reaching lasting success with the Four-Week Quarter goes beyond just having a plan—it requires the right mindset and the determination to stay motivated. A growth mindset helps you welcome challenges as learning opportunities, while a mix of internal and external motivators fuels your journey. While motivation will come and go, building strong habits and resilience will keep you on track. When you combine effort, the right mindset, and accountability, there's no limit to what you can accomplish. Stay patient, trust the process, and watch how the Four-Week Quarter transforms not just how you work—but how you live.

Chapter 6

Measurement Breeds Progress

Why measure?

Dashboard

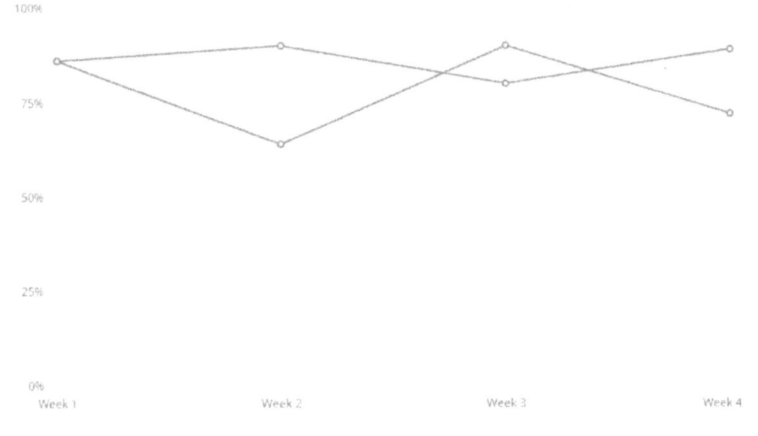

I have two sons, Nick Jr. (8 yrs), and Langston (7 yrs). At a very early age we've always fostered a spirit of competition and leadership amongst the boys. What I didn't know is how these two kids would take it to an infinite level; I swear to you - I heard them arguing about who liked the color green more. With that said they're always wanting me to watch what they're doing; new basketball moves, wild science projects, how fast they can run the bases, how good they can draw, who grew taller this week, etc.; but as the years have gone past in every instance they've gotten better and better and taller. Their constant need for me to watch them do their thing was their form of measuring their performance…."what is measured, is improved".

In the Four Week Quarter measurement is a critical task as it forces us to remain objective about how much our actions match our plans. It forces us to see the truth about who we are and how we're spending our time. It forces a mirror to our true nature as we strive towards what we say we want - only at this time do we truly know our baseline and our beginning of our journey.

We measure because we need to understand how effective we are at following a plan, a plan that based on how we feel about the outcome should give us as much drive as humanly possible to complete. Without performance measurement how would we know how we're doing with our goals? The great thing about the 4 Week QTR measurement process is that we're only competing against ourselves.

Transparency in scoring

In the 4 Week Quarter, the scoring algorithm takes into account goal centered action items, categorical weighted scores, personal daily rankings, and a Q-control score. Since inception of entering the 4 Week QTR program, we've guided you to drill down on your goals, the milestones that make up that goal, and the action items that make up those milestones - at this point there is no getting around taking action on things that will move you closer to your goals.

The weighted categories are based on historical significance of each category as it pertains to the importance specific to completing a goal; those categories are:

- Urgency: how urgent is this action as it relates to the goal you're trying to achieve?

- Impact: how much does completing this action impact your overall goal?

- Duration: how long should this action take to complete?

- Difficulty: how difficult will completing this action be?

Personal daily rankings, where you measure your own performance after each Q-Day from 0% - 100% is the only subjective measure that we allow, but if you're taking the time and effort to complete the 4 Week Quarter program we have confidence that you'll be able to judge your performance fairly and objectively as possible.

Our Q-Control score allows us to protect you against yourself in terms of giving yourself too much grace or judging yourself too harshly. During the process of your weekly review, we ask that you answer four questions regarding that week's performance and lessons learned that we use to feed the Q-Control score algorithm.

Don't move the goal post

It's only natural to lower your goals when things start to get difficult, but in the 4 Week Quarter we account for this natural behavior by having you first understand your most impactful goal, then have you drill down on what milestones make up that goal, and to take it a step further we have you detail those milestones into specific bite-sized action items.

How does this deter someone from lowering their goals? By breaking a large goal into small bite-sized action items, we remove the large looming feat in front of you, we allow you to focus on time-on-task action items that eventually snowball into the large looming goal - anything can be accomplished by completing small chunks at a time.

Chapter 7

Work-Life Integration

"Work-life integration isn't about balancing scales; it's about blending colors to create a masterpiece that looks like your life, not someone else's."

In today's fast-paced world, the line between work and personal life has become more blurred than ever. With technology allowing us to stay connected to work 24/7, it's easy to feel like we're constantly "on." But here's the truth—lasting success doesn't have to come at the cost of your personal well-being. The key to thriving isn't about choosing between work and life, it's about integrating them. Work-life integration means blending the two so you can nurture both without feeling overwhelmed by either.

What is Work-Life Integration?

Work-life integration takes things a step beyond traditional work-life balance, which usually suggests you have to keep your work and personal life in separate boxes. Integration, though, is about finding a flow where work, family, health, and even hobbies naturally fit together throughout your day.

It's not about drawing hard lines but instead aligning your professional and personal priorities so they complement each other. This way, you can shift focus when necessary while still making progress in all areas of life.

The Myth of Balance: Why Integration Works Better

The idea of "balance" can be misleading because it suggests things are always going to be equal, but life just doesn't work that way. Different seasons bring different demands—some weeks your career will require more time and energy, and other times family or personal matters will take priority. Work-life integration recognizes this natural ebb and flow and provides a more realistic, sustainable way to live and work.

Integration means:

- Accepting shifting priorities: It's alright if your focus changes from week to week.

- Blending activities: For instance, you can spend time with family while brainstorming ideas for your business.

- Creating synergy between roles: Leverage insights or experiences from one part of your life to enhance another.

Aligning Professional and Personal Goals

To really make work-life integration work, your professional and personal goals need to complement each other instead of competing.

Strategies for Aligning Your Goals:

- Identify Overlapping Goals: Find ways where personal and professional objectives meet. For example, take a walk during your lunch break to clear your mind and stay physically fit.

- Evaluate Core Values: Make sure your goals reflect what's most important to you. If family time matters, structure your day to make room for it, even during busy times.

- Communicate Priorities: Share your goals with family or colleagues. When those around you understand your priorities, they can offer support without feeling neglected.

- Use the Four-Week Quarter Framework: Apply the same strategies you use to hit career goals to your personal life. Break your personal goals into smaller milestones, just like you do for work, to maintain both balance and momentum.

Creating Flexible Time Blocks

In the Four-Week Quarter system, time blocking is a key strategy for managing work and life effectively. However, life is unpredictable, and strict time blocks can feel too rigid. That's why flexible time blocks are so important.

How to Use Flexible Time Blocks:

- Adjust for Life's Surprises: If something unexpected happens, like a family emergency, shift your tasks to a different Q-Day. Flexibility ensures life's curveballs don't throw you off course.

- Stack Tasks Together: Combine work and personal tasks when possible. Listen to a business podcast while running errands, for example.

- Plan for Buffer Time: Build some unstructured time into your schedule for the inevitable things that take longer than expected.

- Use Theme Blocks: Assign specific blocks of time to focus on different areas of life. Mornings might be for focused work, afternoons for meetings, and evenings for family.

Managing Energy, Not Just Time

Work-life integration isn't just about managing your time; it's about managing your energy. Not all tasks require the same amount of focus or mental effort. Some need you at your best, while others can be tackled during lower-energy times.

How to Manage Your Energy:

- Identify Your Peak Hours: Figure out when you feel the most energized and focused, and schedule your most demanding tasks for those times. Use low-energy periods for easier tasks, like answering emails or tidying up.

- Alternate Between Tasks: Sometimes switching between work and personal activities gives your mind a needed break.

After a tough work session, spending time with family or doing something you love can recharge you.

- Rest Strategically: Don't see sleep, downtime, or exercise as luxuries—they're essential to your productivity. Make self-care a priority in your schedule.

The Role of Technology in Integration

Technology can either help or hinder your work-life integration. On one hand, it allows for flexibility, but on the other, it can make it difficult to fully disconnect from work. The key is learning how to use technology intentionally.

Tips for Using Technology Wisely:

- Set Device Boundaries: Use "Do Not Disturb" modes to create tech-free time, especially during personal or family moments.

- Automate Routine Tasks: Use apps to streamline repetitive tasks, such as scheduling emails or setting reminders.

- Leverage Communication Tools: Use collaborative platforms to stay connected with your team without needing endless meetings.

- Track All Your Goals in One Place: Use the Four-Week Quarter app to monitor your personal and professional progress side by side.

Navigating Setbacks with Grace

Life is unpredictable, and things rarely go exactly as planned. Work emergencies come up, family issues need your attention, and sometimes personal goals get pushed aside. The key to work-life integration is learning to bounce back quickly.

How to Handle Setbacks:

- Practice Self-Compassion: Be kind to yourself when things don't go as expected. Everyone faces challenges; it's part of the journey.

- Reframe Setbacks as Lessons: Look for the lessons and new opportunities that come from unexpected challenges.

- Adjust Goals When Needed: Don't be afraid to modify your goals if circumstances change. Flexibility is key to integration.

- Lean on Support: Don't hesitate to ask for help from family, friends, or colleagues when you need it.

The Importance of Boundaries

Work-life integration thrives on setting healthy, intentional boundaries—not strict rules, but guidelines that keep you focused on what truly matters.

How to Set Healthy Boundaries:

- Learn to Say No: You can't do everything. It's okay to decline commitments that don't align with your priorities.

- Communicate Clearly: Let people know when you're unavailable for work or personal matters. Clear communication prevents misunderstandings.

- Respect Your Time Blocks: Stick to the schedule you've set. If something is planned for Q-Day 1, don't let it spill over into Q-Day 3, especially when that time is for family.

- Review Regularly: Check in with yourself regularly to assess if your boundaries are working. Adjust them if necessary to maintain balance.

Celebrating Small Wins

Work-life integration isn't achieved overnight—it happens in small, incremental steps. Recognizing and celebrating those small wins is essential to staying motivated.

Ideas for Celebrating Progress:

- Keep a "Wins" Journal: Write down your small victories, whether daily or weekly.

- Celebrate with Loved Ones: Share your achievements with family and friends—it makes those wins feel even better.

- Reward Yourself: Treat yourself for hitting milestones, whether it's enjoying a nice meal or indulging in a favorite activity.

- Reflect on Progress: Take time to see how far you've come. Celebrating progress fuels your motivation to keep moving forward.

Work-life integration is not one-size-fits-all. It's a personal journey that evolves as your life and priorities change. Some days you'll feel in sync, and other days might feel chaotic—and that's okay. The goal is to stay flexible and intentional, allowing both personal joy and professional success to thrive.

By aligning your goals, managing your energy, setting boundaries, and celebrating the wins, you'll create a life where work and personal life lift each other up. With the Four-Week Quarter framework, you'll have the structure and tools to achieve this harmony, and with time, you'll realize that a well-integrated life is not just possible—it's deeply fulfilling.

Chapter 8

Using Technology Effectively

In today's world, technology is at the core of how we live, work, and stay connected. But while these tools can help us be more organized and productive, they can also quickly become a distraction if we don't manage them right. When following the Four Week Quarter system, it's crucial that we use technology to enhance our focus and progress, not derail it. This chapter is all about how to make technology work for you—helping you achieve your goals without letting it take over your life.

The Double-Edged Sword of Technology

Let's be real: technology is a blessing and a curse. On one hand, it's never been easier to automate tasks, track goals, and stay connected with people. But on the other, our devices can become constant sources of distraction—emails, notifications, and those ever-tempting social media apps can pull us away from what really matters. The key to using technology effectively is simple: intentional use. You've got to be deliberate about what tools you use, and how you use them, so that they align with your goals rather than derail your focus.

Key Principle: Technology should work for you—not the other way around.

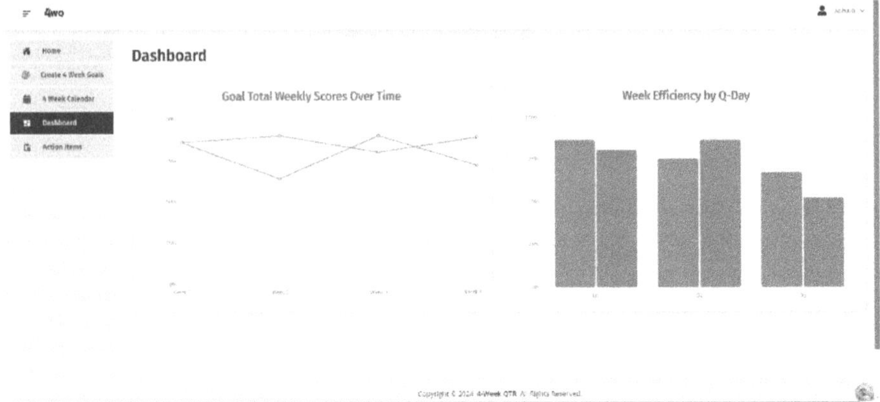

Choosing the Right Tools for Your Four-Week Quarter Goals

There's no shortage of apps and tools out there. With so many options, it's easy to feel overwhelmed or tempted to try them all. But more tools don't necessarily equal more productivity. In fact, too many can clutter your workflow. The goal is to find the right tech that fits your needs and keeps you moving forward.

How to Choose the Right Tools:

1. Identify Your Needs: Figure out what you need help with—whether it's tracking your goals, managing tasks, or streamlining communication.

2. Test a Few: Don't commit to the first app you find. Test out a few options to see which one fits best with your workflow.

3. Stick to Essentials: Use just a few key tools. A good calendar app, task manager, and communication tool should cover most bases.

4. Integrate Where Possible: Pick tools that work well together. For example, sync your calendar with your to-do list to make sure everything's in one place.

Time Management Tools: Staying on Track with Q-Days

Time is your most valuable resource, and that's why managing it is at the heart of the Four Week Quarter. Digital tools can help you stay organized and stick to your Q-Day structure.

Goal-Tracking Apps: Monitor Your Progress Consistently

Tracking your progress is a key part of the Four Week Quarter. You've got to know how far you've come and what adjustments you need to make.

Top Goal-Tracking Tools:

The Four Week Quarter App: This app is tailor-made for this program. It helps track your Q-Day performance, milestones, and overall progress.

Tip: Make it a habit to review your progress every week. That way, you can make any adjustments needed to stay on course.

Communication Tools: Collaborate Without Overwhelm

Communication is essential—whether it's with coworkers, clients, or family. But it's easy to get overwhelmed by the constant flow of messages and notifications. The key is to manage communication in a way that doesn't disrupt your Q-Days.

How to Manage Communication Effectively:

- Slack / Microsoft Teams: These tools help organize work conversations. Set up channels for specific projects to keep discussions focused.

- Email Management Tools (Spark, Gmail Filters): Use filters to sort your emails by priority and reduce inbox clutter.

- Zoom / Google Meet: Use these tools for virtual meetings. Schedule them efficiently, and avoid unnecessary recurring meetings.

- Asynchronous Communication: Encourage people to leave messages rather than expecting immediate replies. This reduces interruptions and allows you to stay focused.

Tip: Schedule specific times in your Q-Days to check emails and messages to avoid constant distractions.

Automation: Streamline Repetitive Tasks

Automation is one of the easiest ways to save time. When used right, it can handle those routine tasks that take up your mental energy, allowing you to focus on what really matters.

Popular Automation Tools:

- Zapier / Make (formerly Integromat): Automate workflows between apps, like syncing your calendar with task lists.

- IFTTT (If This Then That): Use this tool for simple automations, like sending reminders or turning off notifications during focused work periods.

- Calendly / Acuity Scheduling: Automate meeting scheduling so people can book time with you based on your availability.

- Recurring Reminders: Use your task manager to set up automatic reminders for habits or tasks you do regularly.

Minimizing Digital Distractions

While technology can support productivity, it can also be the biggest source of distraction. Social media, constant notifications, and multitasking can all pull you off track.

How to Minimize Digital Distractions:

- Do Not Disturb Mode: Turn this on during your Q-Days to minimize interruptions.

- Block Distracting Websites: Use tools like StayFocusd or Freedom to block sites that waste your time.

- Disable Non-Essential Notifications: Review your apps and turn off notifications that don't require your immediate attention.

- Set App Limits: Use features like Apple's Screen Time or Android's Digital Wellbeing to monitor and limit app usage.

Using AI and Emerging Technologies

AI is reshaping productivity by taking over repetitive tasks and offering insights to improve your workflow. Leveraging AI wisely can make your Four Week Quarter experience even more streamlined.

How to Leverage AI:

- AI-Powered Assistants: Use Google Assistant or Siri to set reminders, manage schedules, and send texts.

- Writing Assistants (Grammarly, ChatGPT): Use AI to streamline your writing with suggestions and corrections.

- AI for Data Insights: Apps like Microsoft Power BI use AI to provide insights into your performance metrics.

- Creative AI Tools: AI-generated prompts can help you brainstorm or overcome creative blocks.

Technology can be a powerful ally on your Four Week Quarter journey—if you use it intentionally. By focusing on tools that align with your goals and minimizing distractions, you'll be able to achieve more in less time and maintain a healthier balance between work and life. Remember, tech is only as effective as the habits and strategies behind it. Keep your use purposeful, review your tools regularly, and don't be afraid to unplug when needed.

Chapter 9

Reflecting on Your Four Week Quarter Journey

As you reach the final hour of the last Q-Day of your Four Week Quarter Program, take a moment to reflect on your journey. Over the past four weeks, you've accomplished a lot:

- Achievement of Goals: You've made significant progress toward your most impactful goal.

- Self-Discovery: You've uncovered insights about yourself that you may not have known before.

- Proven Possibility: You've demonstrated that with effective time management and targeted daily actions, anything is possible.

- Progress Evaluation: Whether you've reached your goal or come close, you've seen firsthand the impact of your dedicated efforts.

- Increased Confidence: You now have a clearer understanding of your goal, your direction, and your progress.

Now, assess your overall completion percentage. Have you managed to hit your daily action items 60%, 70%, 90%, or even 100% of the time? Evaluate how close you are to achieving your target goal.

If you haven't reached your goal yet, don't be disheartened. Look at how much you've achieved in just four weeks. The power of the Four Week Quarter Program lies in its ability to help you accomplish so much in a short, focused period. Now is the time to build on this progress.

I recommend taking the upcoming week to review your findings and refine any new insights you've gained—what I like to call "forced enlightenment." Use this time to ensure that your action items for the next Four Week Quarter are as specific and detailed as possible. With your newfound understanding of your daily schedule, capacity, and targeted actions, you're in a strong position to continue advancing toward your goals.

The Four Week Quarter Program is designed to challenge conventional approaches to goal achievement. By introducing incremental actions, time management, milestones, and measurement, it pushes you to rethink how you approach your objectives. If you've engaged fully with this program, you've experienced genuine growth over the past four weeks. The principles you've applied are now part of your skill set.

Whether you continue to use these tools going forward is entirely up to you, but you now have the knowledge to escape mediocrity and pursue excellence.

The End